with best wishes

best before

Paul Canon Harris

Dedicated to my parents
Cyril (1930-2011)
and Heather Harris
who taught me the power
and beauty of words.

First published in Great Britain in 2012
by Creative Media Publishing Ltd

978-0-9574375-0-0

Designed and produced by
Creative Media Publishing Limited,
35 Woodland Park, Paignton, TQ3 2ST
01803 390569

Introduction

I first started writing poetry because I am totally inept at taking photos. There is a collection in the family albums entitled "Paul's finger goes to Norway" featuring my index finger in every shot! I am a self-confessed people watcher and my poems reflect this. I write about the milestones of life, love, faith, doubt and odd things that make me laugh.

I have chosen *Best Before* as the title for this first collection of poems for a number of reasons. Observational, narrative poetry is, by definition, retrospective in the same way that a photograph captures a particular moment in time. Little poetry is genuinely futuristic or prophetic. What little there is tends to envisage future scenarios that are likened to experiences and settings the poet has known in the past. *Best Before* labels on foods and products link a past creative moment with a point in the future, helping the consumer make a decision (to eat or not) in the present. I recount past events, to amuse, to challenge and inform readers in the present to an extent that it may affect their future decisions.

I confess that I am incapable of resisting a pun or double entendre. As you will see I also love alliteration. Best Before ticks both those boxes. I believe poets are more than a cultural decoration. We have an important role in being a voice on behalf of people whose voices may not be heard, particularly in our current climate of recession.

The poem *Best Before* expresses something of the indignation I feel about the way older people are being treated today.

Central to life is the sense that we are on the clock. To a greater or lesser degree we engage in a battle with time and the ageing process. A recurring theme in this collection is an awareness of the passing of time and the importance of making the most of the time we are granted in life.

I want to thank all my family members and close friends who encourage me in my writing. Special thanks must go to my wife Cathy and to my brother Martin.

I have included a brief section of Notes, either to clarify terms or to give background to the composition where this is relevant.

I hope you enjoy *Best Before*.

Paul Canon Harris
Southbourne May 2012

Contents

Best before

her hand on his arm
love and a lifetime of trust
in her grasp
they make their way slowly down
the aisle

to the cheese counter
where with evident charm
he orders a morsel of cheddar
they will share together

later with a cracker or two
and a milky drink
in matching mugs
dispatched with a playful clink

good health chin chin
down the hatch
try not to get up
too often in the night

they turn to the right
to see what is left
on the bargain shelf
sell-by dates and best-before

bespoke food for those
with failing memories
a weedy border
and shrinking purse

beans, tuna, brown bananas
and a small Hovis
they scrabble for a bargain
their dignity in shreds

he did his national service
they were members of
the "Never had it
so good brigade"

but now
bewildered and betrayed
they find themselves
in reduced circumstances.

Change dodger

Change is persistent.
I am insistent
I do not need her wares.
I already have some.
She hunts me and harries me,
posts flyers through my door
and spams me.
She cold calls and tele-sales.
Ignoring her fails,
for unlike me
she is thick-skinned.
She disturbs meals, matches
and romantic nights in.
I have agreed to browse her
catalogue.
I shall settle for tea lights, a small
table and a rug
to keep her comfortably at bay.

Manopausal Brain

He blew:
fifty candles went out -
instantaneously
the manopausal brain cut in.
Week by week
it strengthened its' grip
on his version of reality.
Young women noticed him in the street,
catching his eye
as he rode by
on his Harley D.
It dawned on him a tattoo
would be fun to do.
His complicit barber agreed;
leaving it longer with highlights
suited him well.
He joined a gym,
took Pilates.
People admired
his air guitar at parties.
A few in the know
stayed silent –
best maintain the status quo.
He began to swim
against a tide
of masculine pride
shot through with regret
as time slipped by.

The Mugging

Our high street
is slightly down at heel.
There you meet
people who are patently real.

Jeremy mutters-
thinks we're all nutters.
Sharon will shout
until she's thrown out
of café or bar.
Last week she stepped in
front of a car.

Phil's selling the Issue -
working not begging.
Old ladies love him –
he's brilliant
at listening.

Pound-shops,
launderettes
and bookies
all have their punters.
Greasy spoon offers
sausage, rashers,
toast and beans aplenty:
All-day breakfast - £1.20.

Hanna's got three kids
and two jobs.
She's Polish
and works in the chippy.
Her English is good
but when she gets tired
she also gets lippy.

People and things
have gone missing.
Hope is slipping away.
We lost
Woolies, legal aid,
respite care and jobseekers
in a recent raid.

Echo headline says
"Police hunt gentlemen crooks."
One kept us talking
while the other
cooked the books.

Hanna blames the Estonians
squatting at number 10.
Phil's sure he saw them,
swears they're Old Etonian.

Meeting Mr Red-Eye

Out they spew
passengers and crew.
Moles appearing
above ground
blinking,making sense
of their new surround.

Escaping from the baggage hall,
runners on the final bend.
Some make a dash
others dawdle,
looking for cash,
buying time,
finding a signal.

Dishevelled
clothes creased,
eyes red,
faces etched
with anxiety
till a sign is spotted
or eyes are met.
Far from cool
this jet-set.

Exaggerated welcomes,
hearty and theatrical.
No film crew here,
paparazzi nowhere to be seen.
Outfits distinctly practical.

Backs are slapped
cheeks are kissed
Mwah! Mwah!
Milk the welcome
as though you were missed.

Excess Baggage

Did you pack this yourself?
No sharp items,
drinks or glass.
Passport,
tickets,
boarding pass.

Step on the scales
behind the recently-departed.
"You're overweight.
I am sad to say.
We cannot carry you today,
you are too heavy-hearted".

11.22 Bournemouth to Waterloo

Two consenting adults
we have read and accepted
terms and conditions of carriage.
We are *advance singles*
despite 30 years of marriage
journeying at a moderate pace
from seaside
through woods and cross heath
to a capital place.

Hinton Admiral-
a smudge of a station,
hint of the nautical
miles from the sea.

New Forest pony
standing lone and bony,
heath, plain,
matted mane.

"Ladies and gentlemen.
This is your train manager speaking.
You can tell from my accent
I was born to more than this.

I will be making my way
through the train
checking your tickets
while you take the... mick."
Good breeding always shows.

Sway – accessed only from the
front three,
not so much a station,
more a stage direction
for hungry souls
heading for the buffet,
grasping hand-holds
left and right,
monkey-barring their way
to over-priced, cling-filmed delight.

I have made eye contact
once too often
with the lady in grey
reading her Kindle book.
Her children play
with hand-held devices
as she gives me a quizzical look.

Container port:
Giant cranes,
like relics of the Jurassic coast -
Behemoths of the Test estuary
emptying leviathans
while upstream anglers
check their flies
and entice the trout.

3-storey flats
grey and drab,
soul-less buildings
spawned by gutless architects
cementing their place
in the hall of shame.

The man across the aisle
knows I am reading his paper
surreptitiously.
He folds it over
before I am done
and looks at me
suspiciously.

"Basingstoke, change for Reading,
Rowlands Castle, the Midlands
and the North."
intones a pre-recorded
sugar-coated voice.

"This train is approaching
Waterloo.
Like us on Facebook.
Follow us on Twitter.
Remember to take all your
possessions with you
and pick up your litter."

All my possessions?
I am travelling light.
Removal vans and a safe store
near platform 4
surplus to requirement.

Stepping on to the platform
travelling clones,
busy drones
vanishing underground,
mobiles to hand,
charging into London's
congested zones.

February

How should I view you,
number 2?
Definitely the shortest
usually the coldest.
January's younger sister
leaping to assist her
at the beginning of the year.

Good things
come in small packages
they say.
Hearts, pancakes, ashes,
not forgetting
my wife's birthday.

I will give you marks for effort,
despite your lack of days,
for being the month
in which days grow longer,
the sun gets stronger,
and golden daffs appear
to mark our ways.

Keep off the Grass

Keep off the grass?
You must be having a laugh,
but then again,
maybe not.

Anachronistic little sign,
nasty bureaucratic whine
from the anally retentive
who are needlessly
over-protective.

I step on your pristine lawn -
tear me off a strip.
You are old-school modernity,
a dysfunctional sign
of the times
laden with negative meaning.
Wordplay in context -
a linguistic puzzle.
Derrida will deconstruct you
then there'll be trouble!
You are a Maginot line.
Canute-like you try
to turn back the tide
of human rebellion.

Grass is for lying on,
loving on
for putting between your fingers
and whistling on,

chewing on,
for sticking on your lip like a joint.
Keep off the grass? – see your point.
Grass is for walking on
for kicking off your shoes and
dancing on.

Prohibition never works.
It simply wakes
a rebel streak
in the recess of our psyche,
and germinates the seeds of sin
lying deep within
the human soul.

Do not try and stop us
pathetic little plaque.
We will have our fun
in the summer sun
and steal you coming back.

Picnics, Pimms and test match special.
A fairy circle beckons me
where the mushrooms can be found.
I slip off my shoes.
This is my summer trespass.
I thank you for it.

Will it rain all afternoon?

Will it rain all afternoon?
asked the girl with a glint in her eye
and a glance at the sky.

It'll stop soon,
said the man suppressing a sigh
looking out of the window at a bus
passing by.

I don't want to miss my friend in the park,
he'll not wait much longer
and the rain's getting stronger.

You'll have to be patient and not
make a fuss,
he'll be there tomorrow if we don't
go today,
now settle down and do as I say.

But he hates being alone
and will cry through the night,
staying here in the warm doesn't feel right.

No more, that's enough.
You'll get cold and be ill.
Please remember he's only a squirrel!

Awake my soul and with the sun

Herring Gull, Cormorant and
I stood,
the water lapping shin high.
We shared a shimmering turquoise
and sky blue meditation.
The rising sun kissed us gently
as a tissue moon ended her shift.
Needles had yet to pierce the
morning mist,
but Old Harry shone to greet
the day
like an exuberant rooster.
Herring gull led a prayer of praise.
Cormorant, raised her wings
in blessing.
I bowed my head and smiled
the Grace.

The Rock-poolers

I see them – still, beyond the sand.
With quartered shirt and floppy hat
one crouches holding pail and net,
while the other stooping stands
with downward gaze and auburn locks.
Brothers hunting among the rocks.

I am not seen – watching from the sand,
as they peer intently in the pool
hands parting silken kelp, salty cool.
Crab and sprat and tiny shrimp
and rocks revealed as tide receded.
Cries of triumph – their quest succeeded.

Now up the rocky path they come.
With gap-toothed smiles and
eager squeals
they speak of sharks and whales
and seals.
Over the bridge and past the swing,
by the stream they free their
meagre catch
and quickly join the cricket match.

Only the dogs make eye contact

This morning I took my smile for a
walk along the cliff top and down onto
the beach.
As we wandered along in the bright
winter sun
we passed women and men,
all shapes and all ages
walking their dogs at various paces.
As each one approached I looked
and I smiled,
nodded and offered my hand to
their dog.
The thing that I noticed, which stood
out a mile,
was how many averted their gaze
and chose not to see.
They say dogs get like their owners
but I cannot agree
for every mutt that I met
made eye contact with me!
Poor humans holding tight to
their leash,
damaged and shy,
stayed well out of reach.

Flotsam, jetsam... and then some

joggers doggers surfers and kiters
swimmers carers scarers and mothers
flashers skaters lovers and haters
all washed up between the breakers.

cyclists artists linguists and botanists
exhibitionists nudists escapists and rapists
fantasists realists bigamists and pessimists
all looking blurred in the sea mist.

singles swingers suitors and rivals
extroverts introverts perverts and experts
relaxation elation vacation and recreation
all thrown together in a sandy location.

side by side on the beach
defying reason and rhyme
within arm's reach
lie goodness and crime
playing near each other
like sister and brother
the beach is a leveler
for a short summer time.

Classic Beach Party

Today we had a wild party on the beac
Thalassa loaned the bouncy castle.
Aphros brought the foam machine.
Helios sorted out the lights.
The sirens called,
the white horses bucked and reared.
And me?
I ran around like an over-excited spanie
my ears blowing back
like the flaps of an old leather
flying helmet.

Returning Tide

There is a moment every year
when the beach changes
character.
Without fanfare or fuss
she is returned to us.
No longer a leisure facility
offering sundry pleasures
under a summery sky,
with high tides and winter storms
she becomes a rugged shore,
a nature reserve once more.

Nkosi Sikelel' iAfrika

God save Africa
from poverty and wealth,
long may she reign
preserved in peace and health.

Scourge her Lord
from Aids and selfish greed,
let her grow in stature
receiving and received.

God save Africa
from war and famine great,
let justice and democracy
be her lover and her mate.

Free her Lord
from burdens of the past,
let the treasures of her history
be the legacy that lasts.

God save Africa
through poverty and wealth,
save her Lord from others
and save her from herself.

(written mid-flight Harare to Nairobi 1.5.91)

Emperor Worship

Smiling down from lamp post,
from kiosk and from cab,
looking down so kindly
like an all-embracing dad.

Such a shame that no-one told
or whispered in your head,
Belshazzar, Nero and Napoleon
have been a long time dead.

Your picture's on the landing,
on the TV and in the hall,
but frankly Mr President
the writing's on the wall.

Nairobi May 1991

High Rise Sunset

Sunset at forty thousand feet
far from pressing crowd and
all-embracing heat.
Shades of the day that's passed,
hues that come and go,
promise of another dawn
to be lived out far below.

Sunset at forty thousand feet
far from pressing crowd and
all-embracing heat.
charms that reach to canvas edge
laid out for all to see,
a visual feast in blue and red,
tongues of fire
spreading dramatically .

Sunset over Zambia 1.5.91

Roadside Smile

Odd split wellington on a happy child
living poor but free,
safe and at ease in this dusty wild.
We wanted to stop and offer you our aid
but sentiments like ours are clearly
"British Made".

What future stands before you
Smiling cattle boy?
Do you dream and plan
or is the present your simple joy?

What have we to offer
as we pass along your road?
Prayers or coins –
anything to lighten our guilty load.

So we gave you nothing,
simply smiled and waved
only to discover on reflection
what an impact you had made.

Forgive us for our smugness,
for our benevolent air.
Thank you just for smiling,
for showing that you care!

Brief encounter on the road from Amboselli –
written at Harare Airport 1.5.91

Victoria Falls Airport Extension

Cosmopolitan, culture-free zones,
full of anxious faces
travelling clones.

East meets west,
and north meets south,
anxiety and tiredness showing
on a multi-lingual mouth.

Freed from imperial duty,
from customs fresh-released,
we wait – the travelling army
purveyors of world peace.

Minute after minute,
year succeeding year
we check the departure board
Ignoring blindly
the nations who have called.

They called on us for justice,
for freedom from war and debt,
for peace.
All we do is negotiate
another airport lease.

Harare Airport 1.5.91

But if he'd written her poetry

If love is eternal
unfettered by the twists of time
then ours is purely primal,
and you, therefore, are mine.
For love knows no order,
gives herself to verse and rhyme,
her passion and her ardour
expose the irrelevance of time.

Through change and chance

I am a wave approaching my love,
unable to turn back
I crash and break.
In calm and storm my destined beach,
all I lack.
Through change and chance
I ebb and flow.
With shingled whisper and breaker roar
I am drawn to her,
my chosen shore.

Don’t wait up

A late night call,
perhaps a text.
Just a single line
“Don’t wait up for me tonight.
We’re playing extra time”.

Such nights don’t happen often,
if they did I know you’d mind.
I’d still stay and watch the game
and be on borrowed time!

At least it’s not a lover
that keeps me up
this late at night.
I’m not a boring workaholic
doing corporate overtime.

Forgive me my obsession.
Humour my misplaced love.
I’ve cheered the boys
through thick and thin -
passion that’s stood the
test of time.

Where the beech leaves fall

I watched them in the autumn wood
among the leaves where the
shepherd's hut stood,
burning with passion, frozen in time,
lost in their feelings, unaware of mine.

She leaned back against the
smooth firm beech.
As he pressed in close, their fingers
reached
between the folds of loosened clothes.
His breathing quickened,
her colour rose.

The softness of skin and lightness of touch
brought smiles to their faces and sighs of delight.
She rested her head against his strong chest,
safe and secure, her heart at rest.
He inhaled her scent and pulled her in tight,

The wind gave a quiver and a leaf slowly fell.
Alive to each other the lovers stood perfectly still.
So gifting them privacy and wishing them well,
I smiled at their pleasure and turned away up the hill.

Indian Summer

Against all odds
and gloomy predictions
in the autumn of her days
the year offered
some warming rays.

Late in the day
in the nick of time,
like finding coins on the street,
blue skies and balmy breeze
arranged to meet.

The change in the weather
was a pleasant surprise,
like love in bereavement,
unlooked for and sudden
when tears are all spent.

So she stopped
and she lingered,
felt the sun on her face
and let the warmth of another
gently diminish the space.

Earthy Holiness

Calluses
Tears
Searing honesty
Swearing words
Acts of kindness quietly done
Greeting strangers one by one

Bruises
Fears
Enjoy parties
Guard secrets
Give away your coat
Enjoy success but never gloat

Blisters
Jeers
Nurture hope
Love with passion
Break the rules from time to time
Be gracious and slow to draw the line.

Window-shopping with Miss World

I followed her down the road,
the grey nun, shoulders hunched
and legs bowed.
Like a scruffy pigeon some fox had
half-mauled
she wore gloom like a cloak
and brown shoes, plain and broad.

Abruptly she stopped at the shop
on the corner,
it was here that I caught her.
She stood peering intently at the
shoes and the slippers.
Sensible styles, imported and piled
in a heap,
little colour, grey and beige,
not cheerful, but certainly cheap.

Just one exception and these
caught my eye,
a pair of pink pumps standing out
from the rest.
I said "Pink ones for you Sister"
and went to pass by.
Surprised she looked up and said,
"They're clearly the best."
I smiled and instantly saw
her face was alight,
her eyes were sparkling and
dancing.
In that moment she was…
Miss World!

You chose me

I did not choose you
football captain,
mercifully
rescuing me
from the frozen line -
you chose me.

I did not choose you
youth club belle,
seductively
dancing with me
out of the blue -
you chose me.

I did not choose you
love of my life,
brazenly
giving me your number
signing my plaster -
you chose me.

I did not choose you
son of man,
lovingly
saving me
from a wasted life -
you chose me.

Remorse

Hindsight is a wonderful thing
I am assured.
So why does revisiting
the scene of my crime,
analysing, reviewing, digesting,
turning back time,
leave me cold with regret and
deeply appalled?

A second bite of the cherry
is what I lack.
A chance to amend, repair and
make good,
but the damage is done.
I dream of returning and
I wish I could.
The tissue of lies was well-spun,
cuffs of chill shame and hot tears
hold me back.

Remorse as a word expresses
captivity well.
The second bite is a sour one that
sticks in my throat,
galling and bitter it blisters my lips
with the taste of regret and words
left to float.
Slowly my past slips by.

Lacking grace and compassion
I languish in hell.

So I refuse the second cup
and the morsel she proffers.
Preferring a home with the weak
I admit my blame and feel at a loss.
Spending time with the broken
and open I seek
the way of the weary, those bearing
the cross,
I throw myself on the mercy the
carpenter offers.

Remission

I am glad
I suppose
to be writing in remission
and not in memoriam.

I write remission,
a single word standing alone,
clearly not a sentence
of indeterminate length;
just a phrase
I am going through
as long as I am granted strength.

A previous generation
understood the meaning well:
blood shed for the remission of sins,
they recited
touching wood and crossing fingers
for heaven;
they lived in fear of hell.

Then the word was positive,
spoke of freedom and life.
Today it reeks of provisionality,
checks my step and scares my wife.

The doctors lay it on me
"Just to cover ourselves.
Best be on the safe side.
Try and take it day by day".

Nothing feels safe
nothing very sure
when you're told your time is
borrowed.
"Don't row too far from the jetty -
your number could be called
tomorrow,
no-one knows anymore".

I try not to think about this all the time,
I know life is a gift.
I've cut the tag around my wrist
and ignore a bucket-list.

Victim fits like a hospital gown.
I wear my own clothes,
smile and hope,
but some nights even the strongest
can feel emotionally down.

At times like that I listen for
the quieter, deeper voice;
a word in the dark saying
"Don't give up,
you still have a choice".

So I press on stubbornly
into another year
determined to live with joy and love
instead of doubt and fear.

Planet Navel

Introspection is something
I have been meaning
to look into
for a while.

I am
galaxy and star,
black hole,
another universe
viewed from afar.

In my cosmos
I do not know if I will
divide
or collide.
Such volatility
challenges my ability
to find
perspective.
My problems are relative -
and my relatives are problems.

In place of radio telescope
I use mirror, bathroom scales
and the odd horoscope.

My Hadron Collider
is sporadic counselling
from a well-meaning friend
I bumped into.
Together we search
the elemental secrets of life.
We explore
anorexia, depression,
medication and meditation.
He gives advice
I ignore.

I am too hard on myself
I suspect.
The only good thing
that can be said
for beating yourself up is
they can't arrest you for it.

Personally
I think
people who think
they can have it all,
do it all, be it all,

who think
they can walk on water
are skating on thin ice
mentally.

In this chaotic galaxy,
the barren landscape of my soul,
I seek a first force,
initial cause,
divine spark
or primary source.
A pin-prick of light
catches my eye.
It draws me.
Travelling deeper, faster,
I fall exhausted,
dazzled, consumed
by the Bright Blur.

Expletives deleted

Flipping heck.
Why the fuss
when I cuss?

For the love of Chomsky.
Don't dismiss me.
Sounds
invested with
universal feeling,
not
offensive meaning.
Judged ribald, coarse,
ignorant and rude
because of the
phonemes
I choose to use.

Expunged, bowdlerized
excised, edited,
and censored,
I could sanitize my speech,
and offer
well-phrased,
beautifully enunciated
gossip.

I know a woman
who swears blind
she'd never curse.
Total vanity
about her
lack of profanity.
Hasn't a good word
to say about anybody-
that's effing worse.

This is not Tourettes
you are hearing.
Simply suggestive alternatives,
artificial additives.
Saccharine language
with the cutting edge
sweetened off.

Killing time

I look like a regular guy
enjoying a small cappuccino and a
sticky bun,
but I
am a highly trained assassin
sitting at a table for one.

On a mission to kill
I sit with an eye on the door
and wait for my quarry.
From under my fringe.
I clock the target
in the crosshairs of my sight,
my finger caresses a steel-cold
trigger.
I have a watch
on my wrist
and time on my hands.

Old Father Time is a slippery
customer:
Master of surprise and disguise.
I rip a month
from his calendar;
he does not flinch.
Relentlessly stubborn
he won't give an inch.
Plenty more where that came from
he smiles.

One day he will
perform his trick and disappear.
Not for a while – perhaps next year.
I won't be around
to join in the applause
I will be somewhere else
in the long pause.

I spend my days killing time
but discover frighteningly,
when all is said and done,
time is killing me.

Your 55th Birthday

London overnight to see a show,
a treat to mark your natal day.
An intermission in a two-act play,
beautifully positioned
a silver celebration away
from thirty and eighty,
astride the midpoint of your life.

Exit stage left: young mother
and callow wife.
Wait in the wings:
old lady who
sings
of autumn shades,
of beauty that fades.
Your moment is now
as you stand centre stage,
assured of your lines
at ease with your age.

London February 2012

Just slipping out

He was
always slipping out
for a newspaper,
a breath of fresh air
or some baccy,
to give the dog a walk,
to see a man about a horse

One morning he just slipped out
and never came back
of course.

Bedford February 2012

Higher still

Flashing crimson, scarlet streak
across a clear blue sky.
Smoking trail and engines shrill,
sound deceiving naked eye,
you disappear behind the hill.
On cliff and beach, children laughing at the thrill
of seeing you and your friends
scream by.
Sandwiches, cold beers and ice
creams consumed,
glances at programmes,
eyes and ears scanning for your
return.

Are they gone? people ask,
sensing an anti-climax,
wanting another pass,
obliviously craving a finish
more spectacular
than the last.

Inland a darker tale unfolds.
Streaking scarlet and trailing
smoke
you brush tree-tops and veer
away from homes.

An open field and river reach -
a glimmer of hope.
Self-less bravery and piloting skill,
stretched to limits, higher still.

There is no return, only impact and
deathly hush.
Whispered rumours quickly
spread;
the word goes round:
a hero is dead.

Bournemouth 20th August 2011 –

Tribute to Flt Lt Jon Egging

All at once it was silent

whirring blades overhead
cutting a Helmand sky
clatter of gunfire around
drip of my
sweat on the ground
orders in my ear
an inner voice
subduing fear
buzzing fly
beating pulse
children's cry
something else
blinding flash
deafening blast
final chance
all at once

it was silent.

Epitaphs – in the Actors' Church

Choosing an epitaph for my dad
Do we conjure the man,
or perhaps the lad?
Many stones and plaques
attempt in line and verse
to capture a loved one's essence
in limerick, doggerel or worse.
Either over-flowery
or painfully terse
Baptised in this church...
buried in this churchyard
Perhaps a little harsh.
Or laughing in the face of death,
not doing things by half.
To be completely honest
I prefer a line that makes
me laugh.
The constant nymph..
She served God right merrily.
Dad for you;
Loving father, faithful priest,
generous friend
will more than do.

Stoke Poges January 2012

Sat-nav Living

At the next request for help:
go straight on.

Prepare to turn left
at the next election.

At the next personal crisis:
pull over
on to the hard-shoulder.

At the end of the month:
you will be overdrawn.

Temptation ahead:
Please make a U-turn.

Sooner than expected
you will have reached
your destination.

Your Majesty – the Regina Monologue!

How should I address you? I wonder
as I take a metaphorical bow.
I understand you are M'am
to rhyme with ham
but if I get it wrong
does it really harm?

Happy and glorious is what we sing,
what we pray.
Grief by definition wreathed
your initial regal day.
You came to power in sadness
when you had barely come of age.
A phone call and a telegram:
a different, larger stage.

We are the new Elizabethans,
we have lived a second golden age.
Now image triumphs over substance:
royals fill many a glossy page.
Is your majesty diminished
By the tv and the press?
In good times and in bad
they have had their pound of flesh.
Reluctantly, inevitably
you have been modernized,
the monarchy rebranded,
repackaged and refreshed.

Like any other family
life has not always gone to plan.
Disappointment, divorce and shame
shared with the common man.
Through the years
with a steadfast sense of calling
you have met each challenge,
passed each test.
Even in your autumn years
there seems little time for rest.
Your personal constitution
is plainly very strong.
I don't know how you cope,
but understand from those who know
you keep a grip on faith and hope.
You are not a towering leader,
on the contrary rather small.
Your integrity, grace and favour
endear you to old and young;
deeply loved by all.

My mother writes to you
to encourage from time to time.
Me? I sing the anthem
and would happily wait in line
to wish you well Your Majesty.
So I thank you on your jubilee
for being a godly queen,
one of the finest
this nation has ever seen.

Notes

Best before 8
The *"Never had it so good brigade"* – from British Prime Minister, Harold Macmillan's famous declaration that "most of our people have never had it so good". This was a speech at Tory rally in Bedford in July 1957 at a time when the country was riding high on the post-war economic boom.

Meeting Mr Red-Eye 14 & Excess Baggage 15
Both these poems were written at Gatwick Airport early one morning while waiting to meet my wife returning from a trip to the USA.

11.22 Bournemouth to Waterloo 16
An account of a single journey – one which I make regularly.

Keep off the grass 21
"Derrida will deconstruct you" – Jacques Derrida French philosopher (1930-2004). He developed the critical theory known as deconstruction. His work is closely associated with postmodernity. *"Maginot Line"* – a long line of defensive fortifications built by France between the two World Wars of the 20th century. Named after French Minister of War it proved ineffective.

Awake my soul and with the sun 24
"Needles" and *"Old Harry"* – chalk cliff formations at the western end of the Isle of Wight and near Swanage respectively.

The Rock-poolers 25
Remembering summers at Castle Haven, Isle of Wight where we spent most holidays as our four sons were growing up.

Flotsam, jetsam ..and then some 27
Beaches are great places for people watchers like me. In this poem I see each word like a person on their towel, in their space adjacent to another.

Classic Beach Party 28
"Thalassa" – ancient Greek sea goddess
"Aphros"- Greek for foam – spirit of the sea foam
"Helios" – Greek Titan god of lights/sun

Africa
I wrote this set of poems while on sabbatical leave in 1991, spent primarily in Kenya and Zimbabwe.

Nkosi Sikelel iAfrika 30
Nkosi Sikelel iAfrika is the title of an African anthem. It was very popular as part of the free Nelson Mandela campaign and the end of the apartheid era in South Africa. Originally composed by a Methodist school teacher as a hymn in 1897, it is now the South African national anthem and includes verses in five different languages.

Emperor Worship 31
At the time of writing I was thinking of President Daniel Arap Moi in Kenya (President 1978-2002) but it has applied to so many world leaders to this day.
Belshazzar: Babylonian king mentioned in Bible. In Daniel Chapter 5 he has a feast in which he sees *writing on the wall* to the effect "you have been weighed in the scales and found wanting".
Nero: Roman Emperor from 54 to 68. In 64, most of Rome was destroyed in a great fire which many Romans believed Nero himself had started.
Napoleon: French military and political leader who rose to prominence during the latter stages of the French Revolution. He was Emperor Napoleon 1 from 1804 to 1815.

Victoria Falls Airport Extension 34
An extension was built at Victoria Falls Airport in readiness for the Commonwealth Leaders' Conference later in 1991.

But if he'd written her poetry 35
The title comes from a conversation between a group of women on an evening out together. One of them suspected her husband of having an affair. She said she could forgive the physical part of the affair but felt it would be all over if he'd written her poetry!

Don't wait up 37
I wrote this on a late train home from Stamford Bridge on 14th March 2012. Chelsea the team I support had beaten Napoli in the second leg of Champions' League match after extra time.

Window-shopping with Miss World 42
A word for word account of an encounter I had in my road one morning.

You chose me 44
Written with one of my favourite Bible verses in mind : "You did not choose me, I chose you. St John's Gospel Ch15 v16.

Remorse 47
This poem owes most to my experience of working with, and being a friend to, a group of ex-offenders, some of whom had to recount their offences on a regular basis as part of their rehabilitation.

Remission 47
An attempt based on personal experience to capture something of the ambivalence associated with being in remission.

Expletives deleted 52
Chomsky: Avram Noam Chomsky born December 7, 1928 is an American llinguist, philosopher, cognitive scientist, historian, and activist. Chomsky has been described as the "father of modern linguistics".

Your 55th birthday 56
Written for my wife Catherine on demand en route to London to celebrate her birthday!

Higher still 58
Written as a tribute to Flt Lt Jon Egging, a pilot in the famed Red Arrows aerobatics team who was tragically killed 20th August 2011 when his aircraft crashed during the Bournemouth air show. I watched his plane head inland over our home seconds before the crash.

All at once it was silent 60
Helmand province, Afghanistan. I had the privilege of getting to know an army captain called "Mike" who did 4 tours of duty in Afghanistan and Iraq as a bomb disposal officer. Hearing how he felt about the men he commanded and lost affected me deeply.

Epitaphs in the Actors' Church 61
Actors' Church: St Paul's Church, Covent Garden, London. My family has long and strong associations with the theatre and Covent Garden. I visit the church frequently and love the tributes to the greats of the theatre and film world. I wrote this poem after one of my trips to our family grave in Stoke Poges – the churchyard was made famous by Thomas Gray's *Elegy Written in a Country Churchyard*

Your Majesty – the Regina Monologue 63
I wrote this poem to mark the Queen's Diamond Jubilee. Despite the tongue in cheek title it reflects my respect and admiration for the Queen. Unbeknown to me until after the event, my mother took it upon herself to send it to Her Majesty. I escaped being sent to The Tower and received an enthusiastic letter and a jubilee goody bag. I suspect my mother omitted to mention I was an adult!